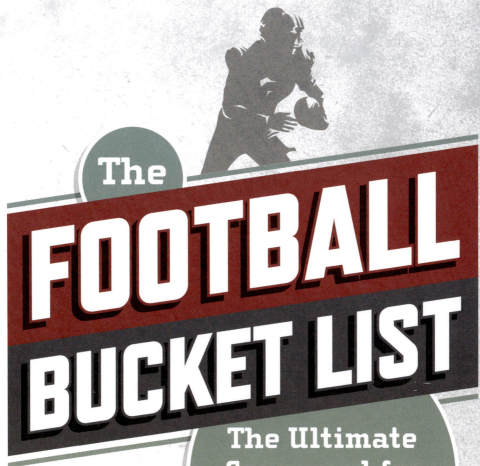

THE FOOTBALL BUCKET LIST

The Ultimate Scorecard for an Epic Season on the Gridiron

Ellen Labrecque

EPIC INK

CONTENTS

How to Use This Journal 4
Travel Tips 5
Football Is Life 6
First Quarter: Best of the Best 8
Second Quarter: Pro Football 16
Third Quarter: College Football 84
Fourth Quarter: The Other Leagues 128
    High School Football 130
    United Football League 136
    Canadian Football League 140
Overtime: The Offseason 144
    Places to Visit 146
    Football Entertainment 152
    Goals and Reflections 156
Stat Sheets 162
Autographs 170

HOW TO USE THIS JOURNAL

This journal serves as a personal record for your football fandom. Throughout these pages, there are prompts to help guide your journaling, but also spots for you to create and capture your own unique love of the sport—whether you write from your couch or a stadium seat. You'll have space to fill in lists of your favorites and specific game-day stats and memories throughout, plus handy stat sheets and autograph pages at the back of the book. Also be on the lookout for "The Playbook" which contains fun football facts and helpful hints to understanding the game.

This journal is divided into four quarters, just like a game:

First Quarter

This section includes lists of football favorites based on fan polls across the country, plus plenty of space for you to fill in your own favorites.

Second Quarter

This section covers everything related to the **National Football League (NFL)**, including major event dates, fill-in pages for every game of the regular season, and other journal prompts to help you collect your memories and favorite moments.

Third Quarter

Gear up for coverage for everything related to **college football**, including all the Division I teams, dates, bowl games, the national championship matchup, and prompts to help you follow your favorite team all season long.

Fourth Quarter

Want to follow other kinds of football besides just the NFL and college? This section is for you! Learn a bit about **high school** matchups, the **United Football League (UFL)**, and the **Canadian Football League (CFL)** and jot down notes along the way.

Overtime

In this section, you'll find tips for must-see football travel destinations, as well as suggestions for stay-at-home football entertainment to enjoy while the game is on break. Write down your favorite books, movies, and other media, and make note of some new ones you want to catch.

TRAVEL TIPS

Most football games can be watched on television from the comfort of your couch. But you might also want to plan some trips around football matchups to get the full experience of the game.

The key to any successful trip—football or not—is to start planning early. You will need to figure out how you want to get there and where you want to stay. And don't forget about grabbing your tickets. Start by looking at the team's website. If you don't have any luck, try resell sites like StubHub or SeatGeek.

If you aren't looking to drop a lot of money, enjoy some of the aspects of football fandom that are free, such as the NFL Combine or the NFL Draft. If you want to travel to some of the biggest high school games in the country, those tickets will also cost a fraction of what you would pay for a professional game, leaving you money for snacks and souvenir gear!

LOCAL TIP

There are some regions where you can catch a college game on Saturday and an NFL game on Sunday. Check out your favorite teams' schedules to see if you can coordinate a trip for when both will be playing at home. Here are five duos to get you started. The stadiums listed are all less than an hour's drive from each other.

Detroit Lions (Ford Field, Detroit, Michigan) and the **University of Michigan Wolverines** (Michigan Stadium, Ann Arbor, Michigan)	**Miami Dolphins** and the **University of Miami Hurricanes** (both play in Hard Rock Stadium, Miami Gardens, Florida)
San Francisco 49ers (Levi's Stadium, Santa Clara, California) and the **Stanford Cardinal** (Stanford Stadium, Stanford, California)	**Seattle Seahawks** (Lumen Field, Seattle, Washington) and the **University of Washington Huskies** (Husky Stadium, Seattle, Washington)

Washington Commanders (Northwest Stadium, Landover, Maryland) and the **University of Maryland Terrapins** (SECU Stadium, College Park, Maryland)

FOOTBALL IS LIFE

America loves football. The pigskin battle is the most popular sport to watch in the United States for people of all genders and backgrounds. In a 2023 Pew Research Poll, 12,000 adult Americans were asked what they thought was "America's sport"; 53 percent of those polled voted for football, while the other 47 percent of the vote was divided among baseball (which took 27 percent of the vote) and other sports. Baseball is called America's pastime, but the polls show that football is America's king.

Superfans don't just watch football. They live it. They breathe it. They paint their faces and stand shirtless for hours in freezing temperatures. I fell in love with the sport myself as a teenager watching my New Jersey high school team battle on the gridiron. The strategy and the physicality of the game were captivating, for sure, but everything surrounding it—the fans, the tailgates, the cheerleaders, the stadium—made it an even more special experience. My family is made up of die-hard Philadelphia Eagles fans (go Birds!). When I was growing up, my mom and dad hosted weekly Eagles parties during the season, serving up a buffet of meatball subs and charcuterie boards for half-time eats. Mutter the letter "E" and my brothers and sister quickly shout out the remaining letters: "A-G-L-E-S! EAGLES!" As an adult, I've worked as a sports journalist and covered some professional football games from the sidelines. Witnessing the strength, power, and athleticism of the players up close made me the superfan I am today.

This guide is filled with pages dedicated to America's sport from a fan's perspective—from our perspective. Want to jot down the details around every week of the NFL or college season? Want to make predictions about future seasons, plan out your fantasy team, or rank the best of the best across various categories? In this journal, there are spots for all of that, and more. And though football has an offseason, you don't need one! During your downtime, you can read, watch, listen to, or play the countless books, shows, movies, podcasts, and video games dedicated to the sport. Or how about taking a road trip to visit an iconic football museum or monument? Players need time to rest and rejuvenate, but we superfans do not.

NFL Super Bowl MVP quarterback Patrick Mahomes once said, "Every experience, good or bad, you have to learn from it." So, you can do what works best for you. Use this journal over the course of one full year or revisit it time and again over longer stretches of time. This journal is designed to help you record all your football experiences—though we anticipate they'll all be good ones!

Let's kick off!

The Playbook

The distance traveled in football is measured in yards. If you measure in meters, quickly convert using this equation: m=yd X 0.9144.

FIRST QUARTER

As a football superfan, you have plenty of favorite things about the game and all the extras surrounding it. What is your favorite NFL stadium? Better yet, what is your favorite stadium *food*? We want you to list all your football favorites in the first quarter of this journal. To inspire you, we also included some favorites as voted on by fans around the US.

| Best NFL and College Stadiums and Food 10 | Best NFL and College Traditions and Mascots 12 | Best NFL and College Players 14 |

BEST NFL and COLLEGE STADIUMS and FOOD

BEST NFL STADIUMS

Lambeau Field
Green Bay Packers

SoFi Stadium
Los Angeles Chargers

Mercedes-Benz Stadium
Atlanta Falcons

Allegiant Stadium
Las Vegas Raiders

Lucas Oil Stadium
Indianapolis Colts

(Source: *USA Today*, 2024)

BEST COLLEGE STADIUMS

Bryant-Denny Stadium
Alabama

Autzen Stadium
Oregon

Tiger Stadium
LSU

Vaught-Hemingway Stadium
Ole Miss

Sanford Stadium
Georgia

(Source: *USA Today*, 2024)

NFL STADIUMS WITH THE BEST FOOD
(and the Best Treat to Get)

Lincoln Financial Field (Philadelphia)
CrabFries

NRG Stadium (Houston)
Barbecue Frito Pie

AT&T Stadium (Dallas)
Chicken-fried Steak

Caesars Superdome (New Orleans)
Jambalaya

Arrowhead Stadium (Kansas City)
BBQ Burnt Ends Mac and Cheese

(Source: Mashed.com, 2024)

COLLEGE STADIUMS WITH THE BEST FOOD
(and the Best Treat to Get)

Bryant-Denny Stadium (Alabama)
Sloppy Fries

Rose Bowl Stadium (UCLA)
Burger on King's Hawaiian Roll

Michigan Stadium (Michigan)
Black Bear Mocha

Amon G. Carter Stadium (TCU)
Beef on Weck Pizza Slice

Ohio Stadium (Ohio State)
Chicago Dog

(Source: *Yelp*, 2024)

MY FAVORITES

BEST NFL STADIUM

1.
2.
3.
4.
5.

BEST COLLEGE STADIUM

1.
2.
3.
4.
5.

BEST NFL FOOD

1.
2.
3.
4.
5.

BEST COLLEGE FOOD

1.
2.
3.
4.
5.

BEST NFL and COLLEGE TRADITIONS and MASCOTS

NFL TRADITIONS

Buffalo Bills
Mafia Table Smash

Green Bay Packers
Cheeseheads

Pittsburgh Steelers
The Terrible Towel

Seattle Seahawks
The Twelfth Man

Chicago Bears
Dressing Like Mike Ditka

(Source: *Allegiant*, 2024)

COLLEGE TRADITIONS

University of Colorado
Ralphie's Run

Ohio State University
Script Ohio

University of Iowa
The Wave

Penn State University
The White Out

University of Notre Dame
Play Like a Champion

(Source: *Sportsnaut*, 2024)

NFL MASCOTS

Indianapolis Colts
Blue

Miami Dolphins
T.D.

Arizona Cardinals
Big Red

Seattle Seahawks
Blitz

Cleveland Browns
Chomp

(Source: *Stay Alive in Power 5*, 2024)

COLLEGE MASCOTS

University of Georgia
Uga the English Bulldog

Louisiana State University
Mike the Tiger

University of Texas
Bevo the Longhorn Steer

University of Oregon
Puddles the Duck

(Source: nfldraftdiamonds.com, 2024)

MY FAVORITES

BEST NFL TRADITIONS

1.
2.
3.
4.
5.

BEST COLLEGE TRADITIONS

1.
2.
3.
4.
5.

BEST NFL MASCOTS

1.
2.
3.
4.
5.

BEST COLLEGE MASCOTS

1.
2.
3.
4.
5.

BEST NFL and COLLEGE PLAYERS

BEST NFL Quarterback
Lamar Jackson
Baltimore Ravens
(Source: NFL.com, 2025)

BEST College Quarterback
Shedeur Sanders
Colorado
(Source: Bleacherreport.com, 2024)

BEST NFL Running Back
Saquon Barkley
Philadelphia Eagles
(Source: NFL.com, 2025)

BEST College Running Back
Ashton Jeanty
Boise State
(Source: Bleacherreport.com, 2024)

BEST NFL Wide Receiver
Justin Jefferson
Minnesota Vikings
(Source: ESPN, 2024)

BEST College Wide Receiver
Jeremiah Smith
Ohio State
(Source: Bleacherreport.com, 2024)

BEST NFL Tight End
George Kittle
San Francisco 49ers
(Source: CBSsports.com, 2024)

BEST College Tight End
Colston Loveland
University of Michigan
(Source: *Sportsgrid*, 2024)

BEST NFL Defensive Player
Myles Garrett
Edge Rusher, Cleveland Browns
(Source: *Sporting News*, 2024)

BEST College Defensive Player
James Pearce Jr.
Defensive End, Tennessee
(Source: ESPN.com, 2024)

WHO DO YOU RANK AS THE BEST?

BEST QUARTERBACKS

1. _____
2. _____

BEST WIDE RECEIVERS

1. _____
2. _____

BEST RUNNING BACKS

1. _____
2. _____

BEST TIGHT ENDS

1. _____
2. _____

BEST DEFENSIVE PLAYERS

1. _____
2. _____

SECOND QUARTER

The NFL season promises awesome touchdowns (and touchdown dances), bone-crunching tackles, and jaw-dropping catches, alongside ample opportunity to spot some famous stars cheering in the stands. Teams battle it out on Sunday or other weeknights, and you can catch the game from home, where you'll get insights from your favorite announcers, or at the stadium, where you can join the excitement of the crowd. Grab your favorite jersey, fire up the grill, and join the huddle—it's go time.

Circle your favorite team(s)!

- Key Dates 18
  - The NFL Scouting Combine 22
  - The NFL Draft 26
  - NFL Training Camps 30
  - Fantasy Football 32
- Regular Season 36
  - The Kickoff Game 38
  - Regular Season Games 40
- The Playoffs 70
  - Wild Card Games 72
  - Divisional Round 74
  - NFC Championship 76
  - AFC Championship 78
  - The Pro Bowl Games 80
  - The Super Bowl 82

- Arizona Cardinals
- Atlanta Falcons
- Baltimore Ravens
- Buffalo Bills
- Carolina Panthers
- Chicago Bears
- Cincinnati Bengals
- Cleveland Browns
- Dallas Cowboys
- Denver Broncos
- Detroit Lions
- Green Bay Packers
- Houston Texans
- Indianapolis Colts
- Jacksonville Jaguars
- Kansas City Chiefs
- Las Vegas Raiders
- Los Angeles Chargers
- Los Angeles Rams
- Miami Dolphins
- Minnesota Vikings
- New England Patriots
- New Orleans Saints
- New York Giants
- New York Jets
- Philadelphia Eagles
- Pittsburgh Steelers
- San Francisco 49ers
- Seattle Seahawks
- Tampa Bay Buccaneers
- Tennessee Titans
- Washington Commanders

KEY DATES

Never miss an important NFL event by jotting down the dates and times here!

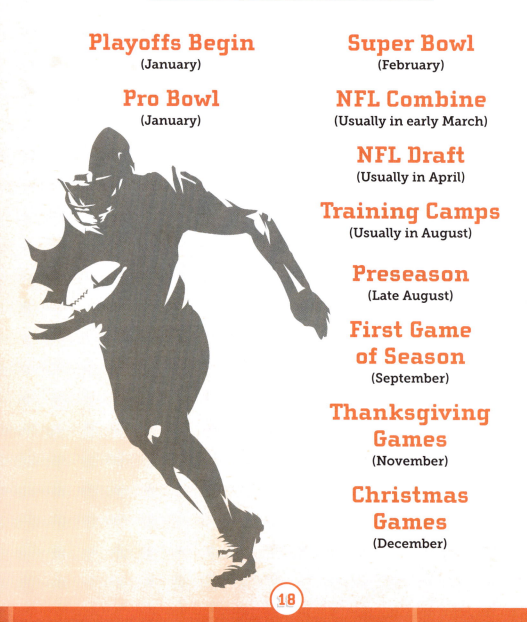

Playoffs Begin
(January)

Pro Bowl
(January)

Super Bowl
(February)

NFL Combine
(Usually in early March)

NFL Draft
(Usually in April)

Training Camps
(Usually in August)

Preseason
(Late August)

First Game of Season
(September)

Thanksgiving Games
(November)

Christmas Games
(December)

JANUARY

S	M	T	W	T	F	S

FEBRUARY

S	M	T	W	T	F	S

MARCH

S	M	T	W	T	F	S

APRIL

S	M	T	W	T	F	S

MAY

S	M	T	W	T	F	S

JUNE

S	M	T	W	T	F	S

JULY

S	M	T	W	T	F	S

AUGUST

S	M	T	W	T	F	S

SEPTEMBER

S	M	T	W	T	F	S

OCTOBER

S	M	T	W	T	F	S

NOVEMBER

S	M	T	W	T	F	S

DECEMBER

S	M	T	W	T	F	S

THE NFL SCOUTING COMBINE

College players strut their stuff in front of coaches, general managers, and scouts from all thirty-two NFL teams at the Scouting Combine. The Combine takes place every year, over the course of several days in late February and early March, during which the teams judge the players' performances to help them determine who they want to draft.

Players participate in physical and mental tests as coaches and scouts evaluate their strength, speed, football smarts, and overall athleticism. Important events include the 40-yard (37 m) dash, the vertical jump, and the broad jump. A player's standout performance can catapult them to becoming a top draft pick, though a bad showing might bury them at the bottom of the list.

How to Attend

Visit nfl.com/onepass to download the NFL OnePass app for more information on registering.

It's free to attend!

How to Watch

NFL.com explains what streaming service you need to watch the Combine on television.

MY NFL SCOUTING COMBINE EXPERIENCE

Dates: _____

Lucas Oil Stadium, Indianapolis, Indiana

The Playbook

Workout Warrior: An under-the-radar player who stuns coaches and fans alike by having a lights-out performance.

Draft Stock: The collective opinion about a player, whether they are going to be drafted high or low. The player's "stock" fluctuates depending on how they perform at the Combine.

NFL COMBINE RECORDS

- **40-Yard (37 m) Dash**
  Xavier Worthy Wide Receiver, University of Texas
  4.21 seconds, 2024

- **Vertical Jump**
  Gerald Sensabaugh Safety, University of North Carolina
  46 inches (1 m), 2005

- **Bench Press (225 lb. or 102 kg)**
  Stephen Paea Defensive Tackle, Oregon State University
  49 repetitions, 2011

- **Broad Jump**
  Byron Jones Cornerback, University of Connecticut
  12 feet, 3 inches (4 m), 2015

(Source: ESPN.com, 2025)

NFL COMBINE PREDICTIONS

Who do you think will have the best stats of the Combine?

40-Yard (37 m) Dash _____

Vertical Jump _____

Bench Press _____

Broad Jump _____

Combine Winners

What were the best stats? _____

40-Yard (37 m) Dash: _____

Vertical Jump: _____

Bench Press: _____

Broad Jump: _____

Whose Stock Rose?
The players at today's Combine who should be drafted higher because of their performance, and why.

_____

_____

_____

_____

Whose Stock Sank?
The players at today's Combine who should be drafted lower because of their performance, and why.

_____

_____

_____

_____

THE NFL DRAFT

Every spring, thirty-two teams huddle up to draft the top college football players in the nation and turn them into pros. The draft is held over three days and includes seven rounds, with each team having one pick per round. The order of the selection is determined by the team's record from the previous season, with the worst teams getting the higher picks and the best teams getting the lower picks.

Best Draft Picks of All Time

Player	Position	Drafted by	Year, Round	Pick
Tom Brady	Quarterback	New England Patriots	2000, 6th	199th overall
Joe Montana	Quarterback	San Francisco 49ers	1979, 3rd	82nd overall
Jim Brown	Running Back	Cleveland Browns	1957, 1st	6th overall
Brett Favre	Quarterback	Atlanta Falcons	1991, 2nd	33rd overall
Roger Staubach	Quarterback	Dallas Cowboys	1964, 10th	129th overall

(Source: NFL.com, 2024)

The Playbook

"Mr. Irrelevant" is the nickname given to the last pick in the NFL Draft.

MY BEST NFL DRAFT PICKS OF ALL TIME

1. _____
2. _____
3. _____
4. _____
5. _____

MY WORST NFL DRAFT PICKS OF ALL TIME

1. _____
2. _____
3. _____
4. _____
5. _____

My NFL Draft Experience

Location: _____

Who did your team select? _____

Are you happy or unhappy with the result? _____

Who Went to What Team

	TEAM	PLAYER
1		
2		
3		
4		
5		
6		
7		
8		
9		
10		
11		
12		
13		
14		
15		
16		
17		
18		
19		
20		
21		
22		
23		
24		
25		

Who Went to What Team

	TEAM	PLAYER
26		
27		
28		
29		
30		
31		
32		
33		
34		
35		
36		
37		
38		
39		
40		
41		
42		
43		
44		
45		
46		
47		
48		
49		
50		

NFL TRAINING CAMPS

Every summer, NFL players participate in training camps held all over the country. R&R is over—it's time to hit the gridiron again. The training camps kick off the NFL preseason. Teams get together to practice, develop team chemistry, install playbooks, and figure out their starting lineup, as well as making some roster cuts. The best part of NFL training camps is that they are very fan-friendly. Fans can attend for free and watch the stars practice up close. It's also an awesome time to get autographs (see page 170 if you need somewhere for players to sign).

Top Fan-Friendly NFL Training Camps

Tampa Bay Buccaneers
Dallas Cowboys
Indianapolis Colts
Green Bay Packers
Los Angeles Chargers

(Source: CBS Sports, 2024)

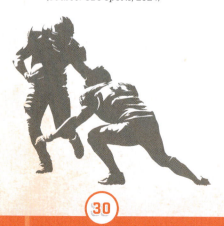

MY TRAINING CAMP PLAN

Date: _____

Team: _____

Location: _____

Weather: _____

Who I Went With: _____
_____

Travel Plans: _____
_____

Unexpected Surprises: _____
_____

Players I Met: _____
_____
_____
_____

FANTASY FOOTBALL

Think you are smarter than an NFL coach? Then try your hand at managing your own team! In Fantasy Football, you draft real NFL players and then earn points for your team based on how these players perform in their real-life games. Your goal is to outscore the other teams in your league.

Tips for Building and Managing a Fantastic Fantasy Team

1. Do Your Research
Stay up-to-date on players' stats and their health.

2. Balance Your Roster
Select players from various positions.

3. Watch for Injuries
Check regularly if any players on your team are injured and adjust your lineup accordingly.

4. Study Matchups
Consider the strengths and weaknesses of your players based on the team you are facing that week.

5. Stay Active
Regularly update your lineup and monitor the waiver wires to pick up new free agents.

Team Notes

My NFL Fantasy Draft

ROUND	PICK	POSITION	PLAYER'S NAME	TEAM	BYE WEEK
		QB			
		QB			
		QB			
		RB			
		RB			
		RB			
		RB			
		RB			
		RB			
		RB			
		WR			
		WR			
		WR			
		WR			
		WR			
		WR			
		WR			
		TE			
		TE			
		DE			
		DE			
		K			
		K			

My NFL Fantasy Draft

ROUND	PICK	POSITION	PLAYER'S NAME	TEAM	BYE WEEK
		QB			
		QB			
		QB			
		RB			
		RB			
		RB			
		RB			
		RB			
		RB			
		RB			
		WR			
		WR			
		WR			
		WR			
		WR			
		WR			
		WR			
		TE			
		TE			
		DE			
		DE			
		K			
		K			

REGULAR SEASON

The air is a little cooler and school is set to begin anew . . . it's football season! The NFL regular season spans eighteen weeks, from early September to early January. Each of the thirty-two teams plays seventeen games with one bye week. Every game counts, as teams try for division titles, playoff berths, and home field advantage, with the ultimate goal being a chance to win a Super Bowl title!

GAME MOST EXCITED TO WATCH

_____   _____
_____   _____
_____   _____
_____   _____
_____   _____
_____   _____

The Playbook — The International Series

Every season, NFL teams play some of their games in other countries. So far teams play in the United Kingdom, Germany, Brazil, Spain, and Mexico. Where is your team going this year?

WINNING PREDICTIONS

Who do you think will be top dog in each division?

AFC East: _____

AFC North: _____

AFC South: _____

AFC West: _____

NFC East: _____

NFC North: _____

NFC South: _____

NFC West: _____

AFC Title: _____

NFC Title: _____

Super Bowl Winner: _____

THE KICKOFF GAME

The NFL Kickoff Game marks the beginning of the new football season. Traditionally held on the first Thursday after Labor Day, the game often features the reigning Super Bowl champions against a top opponent.

THE MATCHUP

_____ vs. _____

Date:

Location:

Weather:

Where I watched:

Final score:

ON THE GRIDIRON

- ☐ Kickoff return for a TD
- ☐ 50-yard plus field goal
- ☐ 60-yard plus touchdown run
- ☐ Touchdown dance in end zone
- ☐ Quarterback scrambles for touchdown
- ☐ Quarterback sack and fumble
- ☐ Interception
- ☐ Defensive touchdown

How Exciting Was the Game?
① ② ③ ④ ⑤

Amazing Plays:

Future Hall of Famers:

Player of the Game:

REGULAR SEASON GAME

THE MATCHUP

_____ vs. _____

Date: _____

Location: _____

Weather: _____

Where I watched: _____

Final score: _____

ON THE GRIDIRON

- ☐ Kickoff return for a TD
- ☐ 50-yard plus field goal
- ☐ 60-yard plus touchdown run
- ☐ Touchdown dance in end zone
- ☐ Quarterback scrambles for touchdown
- ☐ Quarterback sack and fumble
- ☐ Interception
- ☐ Defensive touchdown

How Exciting Was the Game?

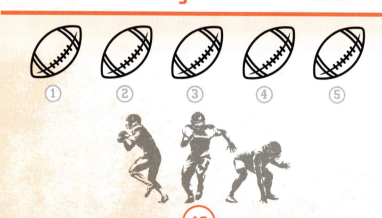

① ② ③ ④ ⑤

40

Amazing Plays

_____

_____

_____

_____

_____

Future Hall of Famers

_____

_____

_____

_____

_____

REGULAR SEASON GAME

THE MATCHUP

_____ vs. _____

Date:

Location:

Weather:

Where I watched:

Final score:

ON THE GRIDIRON

- ☐ Kickoff return for a TD
- ☐ 50-yard plus field goal
- ☐ 60-yard plus touchdown run
- ☐ Touchdown dance in end zone
- ☐ Quarterback scrambles for touchdown
- ☐ Quarterback sack and fumble
- ☐ Interception
- ☐ Defensive touchdown

How Exciting Was the Game?

① ② ③ ④ ⑤

Amazing Plays

_____

_____

_____

_____

_____

_____

Future Hall of Famers

_____

_____

_____

_____

REGULAR SEASON GAME

THE MATCHUP

_____ vs. _____

Date: _____

Location: _____

Weather: _____

Where I watched: _____

Final score: _____

ON THE GRIDIRON

- ☐ Kickoff return for a TD
- ☐ 50-yard plus field goal
- ☐ 60-yard plus touchdown run
- ☐ Touchdown dance in end zone
- ☐ Quarterback scrambles for touchdown
- ☐ Quarterback sack and fumble
- ☐ Interception
- ☐ Defensive touchdown

How Exciting Was the Game?

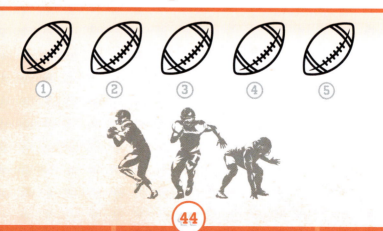

① ② ③ ④ ⑤

Amazing Plays

_____

_____

_____

_____

_____

Future Hall of Famers

_____

_____

_____

_____

REGULAR SEASON GAME

★ THE MATCHUP ★

_____ vs. _____

Date:

Location:

Weather:

Where I watched:

Final score:

ON THE GRIDIRON

- ☐ Kickoff return for a TD
- ☐ 50-yard plus field goal
- ☐ 60-yard plus touchdown run
- ☐ Touchdown dance in end zone
- ☐ Quarterback scrambles for touchdown
- ☐ Quarterback sack and fumble
- ☐ Interception
- ☐ Defensive touchdown

How Exciting Was the Game?

① ② ③ ④ ⑤

Amazing Plays

_____

_____

_____

_____

_____

Future Hall of Famers

_____

_____

_____

_____

REGULAR SEASON GAME

THE MATCHUP

_____ vs. _____

Date:

Location:

Weather:

Where I watched:

Final score:

ON THE GRIDIRON

- ☐ Kickoff return for a TD
- ☐ 50-yard plus field goal
- ☐ 60-yard plus touchdown run
- ☐ Touchdown dance in end zone
- ☐ Quarterback scrambles for touchdown
- ☐ Quarterback sack and fumble
- ☐ Interception
- ☐ Defensive touchdown

How Exciting Was the Game?

① ② ③ ④ ⑤

Amazing Plays

_____

_____

_____

_____

_____

Future Hall of Famers

_____

_____

_____

_____

_____

REGULAR SEASON GAME

THE MATCHUP

_____ vs. _____

Date: _____

Location: _____

Weather: _____

Where I watched: _____

Final score: _____

ON THE GRIDIRON

- ☐ Kickoff return for a TD
- ☐ 50-yard plus field goal
- ☐ 60-yard plus touchdown run
- ☐ Touchdown dance in end zone
- ☐ Quarterback scrambles for touchdown
- ☐ Quarterback sack and fumble
- ☐ Interception
- ☐ Defensive touchdown

How Exciting Was the Game?

① ② ③ ④ ⑤

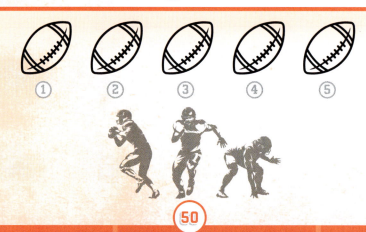

50

Amazing Plays

_____
_____
_____
_____
_____

Future Hall of Famers

_____
_____
_____
_____
_____

REGULAR SEASON GAME

★ THE MATCHUP ★

_____ vs. _____

Date:

Location:

Weather:

Where I watched:

Final score:

ON THE GRIDIRON

- ☐ Kickoff return for a TD
- ☐ 50-yard plus field goal
- ☐ 60-yard plus touchdown run
- ☐ Touchdown dance in end zone
- ☐ Quarterback scrambles for touchdown
- ☐ Quarterback sack and fumble
- ☐ Interception
- ☐ Defensive touchdown

How Exciting Was the Game?

① ② ③ ④ ⑤

Amazing Plays

_____

_____

_____

_____

_____

Future Hall of Famers

_____

_____

_____

_____

_____

REGULAR SEASON GAME

★ THE MATCHUP ★

_____ vs. _____

Date:

Location:

Weather:

Where I watched:

Final score:

ON THE GRIDIRON

- ☐ Kickoff return for a TD
- ☐ 50-yard plus field goal
- ☐ 60-yard plus touchdown run
- ☐ Touchdown dance in end zone
- ☐ Quarterback scrambles for touchdown
- ☐ Quarterback sack and fumble
- ☐ Interception
- ☐ Defensive touchdown

How Exciting Was the Game?

① ② ③ ④ ⑤

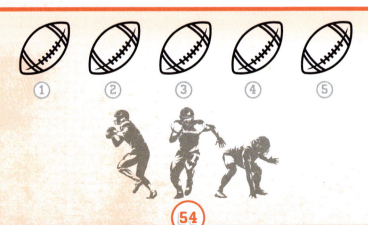

54

Amazing Plays

_____

_____

_____

_____

_____

_____

Future Hall of Famers

_____

_____

_____

_____

_____

REGULAR SEASON GAME

★ THE MATCHUP ★

_____ vs. _____

Date:

Location:

Weather:

Where I watched:

Final score:

ON THE GRIDIRON

- ☐ Kickoff return for a TD
- ☐ 50-yard plus field goal
- ☐ 60-yard plus touchdown run
- ☐ Touchdown dance in end zone
- ☐ Quarterback scrambles for touchdown
- ☐ Quarterback sack and fumble
- ☐ Interception
- ☐ Defensive touchdown

How Exciting Was the Game?

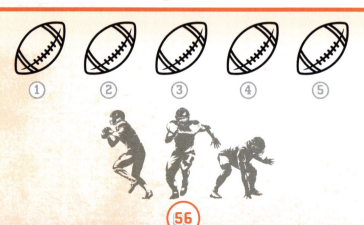

① ② ③ ④ ⑤

Amazing Plays

_____

_____

_____

_____

_____

_____

Future Hall of Famers

_____

_____

_____

_____

_____

_____

REGULAR SEASON GAME

★ THE MATCHUP ★

_____ vs. _____

Date: _____

Location: _____

Weather: _____

Where I watched: _____

Final score: _____

ON THE GRIDIRON

☐ Kickoff return for a TD
☐ 50-yard plus field goal
☐ 60-yard plus touchdown run
☐ Touchdown dance in end zone
☐ Quarterback scrambles for touchdown
☐ Quarterback sack and fumble
☐ Interception
☐ Defensive touchdown

How Exciting Was the Game?

🏈 ① 🏈 ② 🏈 ③ 🏈 ④ 🏈 ⑤

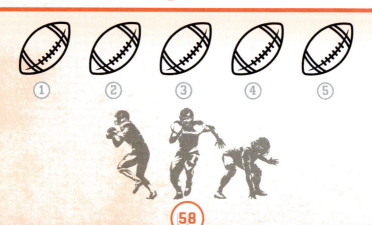

58

Amazing Plays

_____

_____

_____

_____

_____

Future Hall of Famers

_____

_____

_____

_____

REGULAR SEASON GAME

★ THE MATCHUP ★

_____ vs. _____

Date:

Location:

Weather:

Where I watched:

Final score:

ON THE GRIDIRON

- ☐ Kickoff return for a TD
- ☐ 50-yard plus field goal
- ☐ 60-yard plus touchdown run
- ☐ Touchdown dance in end zone
- ☐ Quarterback scrambles for touchdown
- ☐ Quarterback sack and fumble
- ☐ Interception
- ☐ Defensive touchdown

How Exciting Was the Game?

① ② ③ ④ ⑤

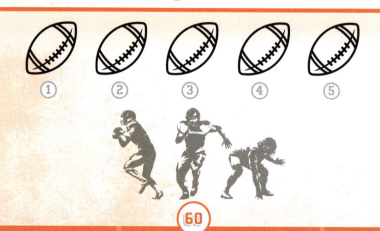

Amazing Plays

_____

_____

_____

_____

_____

_____

Future Hall of Famers

_____

_____

_____

_____

REGULAR SEASON GAME

THE MATCHUP

_____ vs. _____

Date: _____

Location: _____

Weather: _____

Where I watched: _____

Final score: _____

ON THE GRIDIRON

- ☐ Kickoff return for a TD
- ☐ 50-yard plus field goal
- ☐ 60-yard plus touchdown run
- ☐ Touchdown dance in end zone
- ☐ Quarterback scrambles for touchdown
- ☐ Quarterback sack and fumble
- ☐ Interception
- ☐ Defensive touchdown

How Exciting Was the Game?

① ② ③ ④ ⑤

Amazing Plays

_____

_____

_____

_____

_____

Future Hall of Famers

_____

_____

_____

_____

REGULAR SEASON GAME

★ THE MATCHUP ★

_____ vs. _____

Date:

Location:

Weather:

Where I watched:

Final score:

ON THE GRIDIRON

- ☐ Kickoff return for a TD
- ☐ 50-yard plus field goal
- ☐ 60-yard plus touchdown run
- ☐ Touchdown dance in end zone
- ☐ Quarterback scrambles for touchdown
- ☐ Quarterback sack and fumble
- ☐ Interception
- ☐ Defensive touchdown

How Exciting Was the Game?

① ② ③ ④ ⑤

Amazing Plays

_____
_____
_____
_____
_____

Future Hall of Famers

_____
_____
_____
_____

REGULAR SEASON GAME

THE MATCHUP

_____ vs. _____

Date:

Location:

Weather:

Where I watched:

Final score:

ON THE GRIDIRON

- [ ] Kickoff return for a TD
- [ ] 50-yard plus field goal
- [ ] 60-yard plus touchdown run
- [ ] Touchdown dance in end zone
- [ ] Quarterback scrambles for touchdown
- [ ] Quarterback sack and fumble
- [ ] Interception
- [ ] Defensive touchdown

How Exciting Was the Game?

① ② ③ ④ ⑤

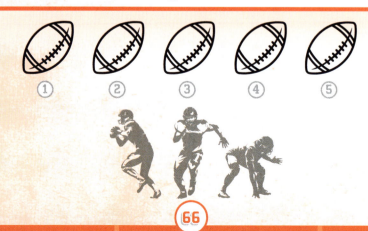

Amazing Plays

_____

_____

_____

_____

_____

Future Hall of Famers

_____

_____

_____

_____

REGULAR SEASON GAME

THE MATCHUP

_____ vs. _____

Date:

Location:

Weather:

Where I watched:

Final score:

ON THE GRIDIRON

- ☐ Kickoff return for a TD
- ☐ 50-yard plus field goal
- ☐ 60-yard plus touchdown run
- ☐ Touchdown dance in end zone
- ☐ Quarterback scrambles for touchdown
- ☐ Quarterback sack and fumble
- ☐ Interception
- ☐ Defensive touchdown

How Exciting Was the Game?

① ② ③ ④ ⑤

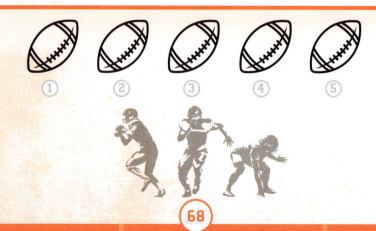

Amazing Plays

_____
_____
_____
_____
_____

Future Hall of Famers

_____
_____
_____
_____

THE PLAYOFFS

The regular season has concluded, which means it's time to fill in our playoff bracket! You can either use this bracket to predict the winners or fill it in as the playoffs unfold—or both!

CHAMPIONS

CONFERENCE CHAMPIONSHIP	DIVISIONAL ROUND	WILD CARD

NFC

1.
4.
5.
3.
6.
2.
7.

WILD CARD GAMES

The Wild Card Games are the first six games played in the NFL postseason. The winners of each game advance to the Divisional Round. The Wild Card Games are arranged by seeding—for example, the lowest-ranked seed faces the highest-ranked seed. Additionally, the higher seed receives a home field advantage for the game.

_____ vs. _____   Location: _____

Date: _____   Where I watched: _____

Weather: _____   **How Exciting Was the Game?**

Final score: _____   ① ② ③ ④ ⑤

_____ vs. _____   Location: _____

Date: _____   Where I watched: _____

Weather: _____   **How Exciting Was the Game?**

Final score: _____   ① ② ③ ④ ⑤

_____ vs. _____   Location: _____

Date: _____   Where I watched: _____

Weather: _____   **How Exciting Was the Game?**

Final score: _____   ① ② ③ ④ ⑤

_____ vs. _____   Location: _____

Date: _____   Where I watched: _____

Weather: _____   **How Exciting Was the Game?**

Final score: _____   ① ② ③ ④ ⑤

_____ vs. _____   Location: _____

Date: _____   Where I watched: _____

Weather: _____   **How Exciting Was the Game?**

Final score: _____   ① ② ③ ④ ⑤

_____ vs. _____   Location: _____

Date: _____   Where I watched: _____

Weather: _____   **How Exciting Was the Game?**

Final score: _____   ① ② ③ ④ ⑤

DIVISIONAL ROUND

The Divisional Round includes the three Wild Card winners and the number one seed from each conference (top teams that had a bye in the Wild Card round). Four games are played—two in each conference—with the winners moving on to the Conference Championships.

_____ vs. _____

Location: _____

Date: _____

Where I watched: _____

Weather: _____

Final score: _____

PLAYER OF THE GAME _____

How Exciting Was the Game?
① ② ③ ④ ⑤

_____ vs. _____

Location: _____

Date: _____

Where I watched: _____

Weather: _____

Final score: _____

PLAYER OF THE GAME _____

How Exciting Was the Game?
① ② ③ ④ ⑤

_____ vs. _____   Location: _____

Date: _____   Where I watched: _____

Weather: _____   Final score: _____

PLAYER OF THE GAME _____

How Exciting Was the Game?
① ② ③ ④ ⑤

_____ vs. _____   Location: _____

Date: _____   Where I watched: _____

Weather: _____   Final score: _____

PLAYER OF THE GAME _____

How Exciting Was the Game?
① ② ③ ④ ⑤

★★★ NFC CHAMPIONSHIP ★★★

The NFC Championship is one of the two semifinal playoff games. The winner moves on to the biggest show of all—the Super Bowl.

THE MATCHUP

_____ vs. _____

Date: _____

Location: _____

Weather: _____

Where I watched: _____

Final score: _____

ON THE GRIDIRON

- ☐ Kickoff return for a TD
- ☐ 50-yard plus field goal
- ☐ 60-yard plus touchdown run
- ☐ Touchdown dance in end zone
- ☐ Quarterback scrambles for touchdown
- ☐ Quarterback sack and fumble
- ☐ Interception
- ☐ Defensive touchdown

How Exciting Was the Game?
① ② ③ ④ ⑤

Amazing Plays:

Future Hall of Famers:

Player of the Game:

★★★ AFC CHAMPIONSHIP ★★★

The AFC Championship is the other semifinal playoff game. The winner of this game faces the winner of the NFC Championship game in the Super Bowl.

THE MATCHUP

_____ vs. _____

Date: _____

Location: _____

Weather: _____

Where I watched: _____

Final score: _____

ON THE GRIDIRON

- ☐ Kickoff return for a TD
- ☐ 50-yard plus field goal
- ☐ 60-yard plus touchdown run
- ☐ Touchdown dance in end zone
- ☐ Quarterback scrambles for touchdown
- ☐ Quarterback sack and fumble
- ☐ Interception
- ☐ Defensive touchdown

How Exciting Was the Game?

① ② ③ ④ ⑤

Amazing Plays:

Future Hall of Famers:

Player of the Game:

THE PRO BOWL GAMES

The Pro Bowl Games are the NFL's annual all-star competition featuring the best players from the league's two conferences. The Games are usually played a week before the Super Bowl. The players included are voted on by fans, coaches, and players. Since 2022, the Games have included a noncontact flag football game and other matchups, including passing and kicking competitions and even a dodgeball showdown.

Location:

Top offensive player of the flag football game:

Top defensive player of the flag football game:

Competition winners:

Best Moments of the Pro Bowl

THE SUPER BOWL

The Super Bowl is the most watched event in all of American sports, pitting the AFC champion against the NFC champion. The game is thrilling in and of itself, but add in high-profile commercials and an elaborate half-time show and you get an unbeatable experience. (And we haven't even mentioned the incredible menu that usually accompanies most watch parties!)

As of 2024, the Pittsburgh Steelers and the New England Patriots are tied for the most titles (6), but the Patriots have appeared in the game the most times (11). Is your team going to win it this year?

_____ vs. _____

Date: _____ **Location:** _____

Where I watched: _____ **Weather:** _____

Who I watched with: _____

_____

What I ate: _____

_____

Best commercial: _____

Best TD celebration: _____

How Exciting Was the Game?

① ② ③ ④ ⑤

The Halftime Show  or

_____
_____
_____
_____
_____

 _____

The Playbook

The Super Bowl uses Roman numerals to avoid confusion, because the NFL season takes place in two different years.

Lamar Hunt, who owned the Kansas City Chiefs, came up with the championship name. His kids were playing with a toy called a Super Ball—so he decided to name the game the Super Bowl! (Source: USA Today)

Miami, Florida, and New Orleans, Louisiana, have hosted the most Super Bowls, with 11 each as of 2025. (Source: CBS Sports)

THIRD QUARTER

The college football season is played at about the same time as the NFL season, running from late August through early January. There are 128 Division I teams and ten different conferences. College football game-day atmosphere is electrifying! Each game includes tailgates, marching band halftime shows, and some of the most fervent fans in all of sports. Grab your team's foam finger and paint your face! Let's dig into the season.

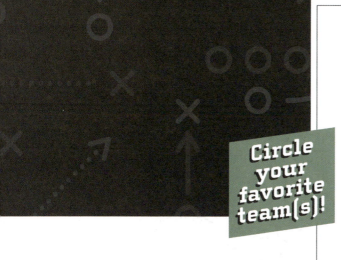

College Division I Teams

Atlantic Coast Conference (ACC)
Boston College
California (Cal)
Clemson
Duke
Florida State
Georgia Tech
Louisville
Miami
North Carolina
North Carolina State
Pittsburgh
Southern Methodist
Stanford
Syracuse
Virginia
Virginia Tech
Wake Forest

American Athletic Conference (AAC)
Charlotte
East Carolina
Florida Atlantic
Memphis
Navy
North Texas
Rice
South Florida
Temple
Tulane
Tulsa
University of Alabama at Birmingham
University of Texas at San Antonio

(coninued on next page)

Key Dates	88
Regular Season	92
College Playoffs	118
Quarterfinals And Semifinals	122
National Championship Game	126
College Award Winners	127

(continued from previous page)

Big 12 Conference
Arizona
Arizona State
Baylor
Brigham Young
Cincinnati
Colorado
Houston
Iowa State
Kansas
Kansas State
Oklahoma State
Texas Christian
Texas Tech
University of Central Florida
Utah
West Virginia

Big Ten Conference
Illinois
Indiana
Iowa
Maryland
Michigan
Michigan State
Minnesota
Nebraska
Northwestern
Ohio State
Oregon
Penn State
Purdue
Rutgers
UCLA
USC
Washington
Wisconsin

Conference USA (C-USA)
FIU
Jacksonville State
Kennesaw State
Liberty
Louisiana Tech
Middle Tennessee
New Mexico State
Sam Houston
UTEP
Western Kentucky

Mid-American Conference (MAC)
Akron
Ball State
Bowling Green
Buffalo
Central Michigan
Eastern Michigan
Kent State
Miami (Ohio)
Northern Illinois
Ohio
Toledo
Western Michigan

Mountain West Conference
Air Force
Boise State
Colorado State
Fresno State
Hawaii
Nevada
New Mexico
San Diego State
San Jose State
UNLV
Utah State
Wyoming

Pac-12 Conference
Oregon State
Washington State

Southeastern Conference (SEC)
Alabama
Arkansas
Auburn
Florida
Georgia
Kentucky
LSU
Mississippi State
Missouri
Oklahoma
Ole Miss
South Carolina
Tennessee
Texas
Texas A&M
Vanderbilt

Sun Belt Conference
Appalachian State
Arkansas State
Coastal Carolina
Georgia Southern
Georgia State
James Madison
Louisiana
Marshall
Old Dominion
South Alabama
Southern Miss
Texas State
Troy
ULM (Louisiana-Monroe)

Independents
Army
Notre Dame
UConn
UMass

KEY DATES

Never miss an important college event by jotting down the dates and times here!

Championship Game
(January)

Signing Day
(February)

Training Camps
(August)

First Game of Season
(August)

NCAA Playoffs
(December)

JANUARY

S	M	T	W	T	F	S

FEBRUARY

S	M	T	W	T	F	S

MARCH

S	M	T	W	T	F	S

APRIL

S	M	T	W	T	F	S

MAY

S	M	T	W	T	F	S

JUNE

S	M	T	W	T	F	S

JULY

S	M	T	W	T	F	S

AUGUST

S	M	T	W	T	F	S

SEPTEMBER

S	M	T	W	T	F	S

OCTOBER

S	M	T	W	T	F	S

NOVEMBER

S	M	T	W	T	F	S

DECEMBER

S	M	T	W	T	F	S

REGULAR SEASON

During the regular college season, teams face opponents both within and outside their conference. The regular season lasts 12 to 13 weeks and every game counts, with a win raising a team's ranking and a loss lowering it.

The Associated Press provides weekly rankings for the top twenty-five NCAA Division I FBS football teams—but what are your own rankings? Fill in your own top twenty-five here.

My Top Rankings

1. _____

2. _____

3. _____

4. _____

5. _____

6. _____

7. _____

8. _____

9. _____

10. _____

11. _____

12. _____
13. _____
14. _____
15. _____
16. _____
17. _____
18. _____
19. _____
20. _____
21. _____
22. _____
23. _____
24. _____
25. _____

REGULAR SEASON GAME

★ THE MATCHUP ★

_____ vs. _____

Date:

Location:

Weather:

Where I watched:

Final score:

ON THE GRIDIRON

- Kickoff return for a TD
- 50-yard plus field goal
- 60-yard plus touchdown run
- Touchdown dance in end zone
- Quarterback scrambles for touchdown
- Quarterback sack and fumble
- Interception
- Defensive touchdown

How Exciting Was the Game?

① ② ③ ④ ⑤

94

Amazing Plays: _____

_____

_____

_____

Future NFL Players: _____

_____

_____

Coolest Mascot: _____

_____

Best Tailgating Traditions: _____

_____

REGULAR SEASON GAME

★ THE MATCHUP ★

_____ vs. _____

Date: _____

Location: _____

Weather: _____

Where I watched: _____

Final score: _____

ON THE GRIDIRON

☐ Kickoff return for a TD
☐ 50-yard plus field goal
☐ 60-yard plus touchdown run
☐ Touchdown dance in end zone
☐ Quarterback scrambles for touchdown
☐ Quarterback sack and fumble
☐ Interception
☐ Defensive touchdown

How Exciting Was the Game?

① ② ③ ④ ⑤

Amazing Plays: _____

_____

_____

Future NFL Players: _____

_____

_____

Coolest Mascot: _____

_____

Best Tailgating Traditions: _____

_____

REGULAR SEASON GAME

★ THE MATCHUP ★

_____ vs. _____

Date: _____

Location: _____

Weather: _____

Where I watched: _____

Final score: _____

ON THE GRIDIRON

☐ Kickoff return for a TD
☐ 50-yard plus field goal
☐ 60-yard plus touchdown run
☐ Touchdown dance in end zone
☐ Quarterback scrambles for touchdown
☐ Quarterback sack and fumble
☐ Interception
☐ Defensive touchdown

How Exciting Was the Game?

① ② ③ ④ ⑤

Amazing Plays: _____

_____

_____

_____

Future NFL Players: _____

_____

_____

Coolest Mascot: _____

_____

Best Tailgating Traditions: _____

_____

REGULAR SEASON GAME

★ THE MATCHUP ★

_____ vs. _____

Date: _____

Location: _____

Weather: _____

Where I watched: _____

Final score: _____

ON THE GRIDIRON

- ☐ Kickoff return for a TD
- ☐ 50-yard plus field goal
- ☐ 60-yard plus touchdown run
- ☐ Touchdown dance in end zone
- ☐ Quarterback scrambles for touchdown
- ☐ Quarterback sack and fumble
- ☐ Interception
- ☐ Defensive touchdown

How Exciting Was the Game?

① ② ③ ④ ⑤

100

Amazing Plays: _____

_____

_____

Future NFL Players: _____

_____

_____

Coolest Mascot: _____

_____

Best Tailgating Traditions: _____

_____

REGULAR SEASON GAME

★ THE MATCHUP ★

_____ vs. _____

Date:

Location:

Weather:

Where I watched:

Final score:

ON THE GRIDIRON

- ☐ Kickoff return for a TD
- ☐ 50-yard plus field goal
- ☐ 60-yard plus touchdown run
- ☐ Touchdown dance in end zone
- ☐ Quarterback scrambles for touchdown
- ☐ Quarterback sack and fumble
- ☐ Interception
- ☐ Defensive touchdown

How Exciting Was the Game?

🏈 ① 🏈 ② 🏈 ③ 🏈 ④ 🏈 ⑤

102

Amazing Plays: _____

_____

_____

_____

Future NFL Players: _____

_____

_____

Coolest Mascot: _____

_____

Best Tailgating Traditions: _____

_____

REGULAR SEASON GAME

★ THE MATCHUP ★

_____ vs. _____

Date:

Location:

Weather:

Where I watched:

Final score:

ON THE GRIDIRON

- ☐ Kickoff return for a TD
- ☐ 50-yard plus field goal
- ☐ 60-yard plus touchdown run
- ☐ Touchdown dance in end zone
- ☐ Quarterback scrambles for touchdown
- ☐ Quarterback sack and fumble
- ☐ Interception
- ☐ Defensive touchdown

How Exciting Was the Game?

① ② ③ ④ ⑤

Amazing Plays: _____

_____

_____

_____

Future NFL Players: _____

_____

_____

Coolest Mascot: _____

_____

Best Tailgating Traditions: _____

_____

REGULAR SEASON GAME

THE MATCHUP

_____ vs. _____

Date: _____

Location: _____

Weather: _____

Where I watched: _____

Final score: _____

ON THE GRIDIRON

- ☐ Kickoff return for a TD
- ☐ 50-yard plus field goal
- ☐ 60-yard plus touchdown run
- ☐ Touchdown dance in end zone
- ☐ Quarterback scrambles for touchdown
- ☐ Quarterback sack and fumble
- ☐ Interception
- ☐ Defensive touchdown

How Exciting Was the Game?

① ② ③ ④ ⑤

Amazing Plays: _____

_____

_____

_____

Future NFL Players: _____

_____

_____

Coolest Mascot: _____

_____

Best Tailgating Traditions: _____

_____

REGULAR SEASON GAME

★ THE MATCHUP ★

_____ vs. _____

Date:

Location:

Weather:

Where I watched:

Final score:

ON THE GRIDIRON

- ☐ Kickoff return for a TD
- ☐ 50-yard plus field goal
- ☐ 60-yard plus touchdown run
- ☐ Touchdown dance in end zone
- ☐ Quarterback scrambles for touchdown
- ☐ Quarterback sack and fumble
- ☐ Interception
- ☐ Defensive touchdown

How Exciting Was the Game?

① ② ③ ④ ⑤

108

Amazing Plays: _____

_____

_____

_____

Future NFL Players: _____

_____

_____

Coolest Mascot: _____

_____

Best Tailgating Traditions: _____

_____

REGULAR SEASON GAME

★ THE MATCHUP ★

_____ vs. _____

Date: _____

Location: _____

Weather: _____

Where I watched: _____

Final score: _____

ON THE GRIDIRON

☐ Kickoff return for a TD
☐ 50-yard plus field goal
☐ 60-yard plus touchdown run
☐ Touchdown dance in end zone
☐ Quarterback scrambles for touchdown
☐ Quarterback sack and fumble
☐ Interception
☐ Defensive touchdown

How Exciting Was the Game?

① ② ③ ④ ⑤

Amazing Plays: _____

_____

_____

_____

Future NFL Players: _____

_____

_____

Coolest Mascot: _____

_____

Best Tailgating Traditions: _____

_____

REGULAR SEASON GAME

★ THE MATCHUP ★

_____ vs. _____

Date:

Location:

Weather:

Where I watched:

Final score:

ON THE GRIDIRON

- ☐ Kickoff return for a TD
- ☐ 50-yard plus field goal
- ☐ 60-yard plus touchdown run
- ☐ Touchdown dance in end zone
- ☐ Quarterback scrambles for touchdown
- ☐ Quarterback sack and fumble
- ☐ Interception
- ☐ Defensive touchdown

How Exciting Was the Game?

① ② ③ ④ ⑤

Amazing Plays: _____

_____

_____

_____

Future NFL Players: _____

_____

_____

Coolest Mascot: _____

_____

Best Tailgating Traditions: _____

_____

REGULAR SEASON GAME

★ THE MATCHUP ★

_____ vs. _____

Date:

Location:

Weather:

Where I watched:

Final score:

ON THE GRIDIRON

- Kickoff return for a TD
- 50-yard plus field goal
- 60-yard plus touchdown run
- Touchdown dance in end zone
- Quarterback scrambles for touchdown
- Quarterback sack and fumble
- Interception
- Defensive touchdown

How Exciting Was the Game?

① ② ③ ④ ⑤

Amazing Plays: _____
_____
_____
_____

Future NFL Players: _____
_____
_____
_____

Coolest Mascot: _____
_____

Best Tailgating Traditions: _____
_____

REGULAR SEASON GAME

THE MATCHUP

_____ vs. _____

Date: _____

Location: _____

Weather: _____

Where I watched: _____

Final score: _____

ON THE GRIDIRON

☐ Kickoff return for a TD
☐ 50-yard plus field goal
☐ 60-yard plus touchdown run
☐ Touchdown dance in end zone
☐ Quarterback scrambles for touchdown
☐ Quarterback sack and fumble
☐ Interception
☐ Defensive touchdown

How Exciting Was the Game?

① ② ③ ④ ⑤

116

Amazing Plays: _____
_____
_____
_____

Future NFL Players: _____
_____
_____
_____

Coolest Mascot: _____
_____

Best Tailgating Traditions: _____
_____

COLLEGE PLAYOFFS

The college football postseason has arrived and beginning in 2024, the top 12 teams have been selected for the playoffs (previously, only the top four teams made it). Champions from four top conferences receive first round byes, meaning they don't have to play that round. Teams 5–12 will play each other (the higher-team seed has a home field advantage). The quarterfinal and the semifinal games rotate between six traditional bowl games, while the national title game is played at a different neutral site every year.

The 12-team playoff gives automatic bids to the champions from the five highest-ranked conferences. The next seven highest-ranked teams fill in the rest of the spots on the bracket. The top four teams receive a first-round bye to the quarterfinals.

Fill in the following pages with your predictions and the teams that make the cut.

WINNING PREDICTIONS

Who do you think will be the top team in each conference?

Big 12 Conference: _____

Big Ten Conference: _____

Conference USA
(C-USA): _____

Mid-American
Conference (MAC): _____

Mountain West
Conference: _____

Pac-12 Conference: _____

Southeastern
Conference (SEC): _____

Sun Belt Conference: _____

National Champion: _____

The regular season has concluded, which means it's time to fill in our playoff bracket! You can either use this bracket to predict the winners or fill it in as the playoffs unfold—or both!

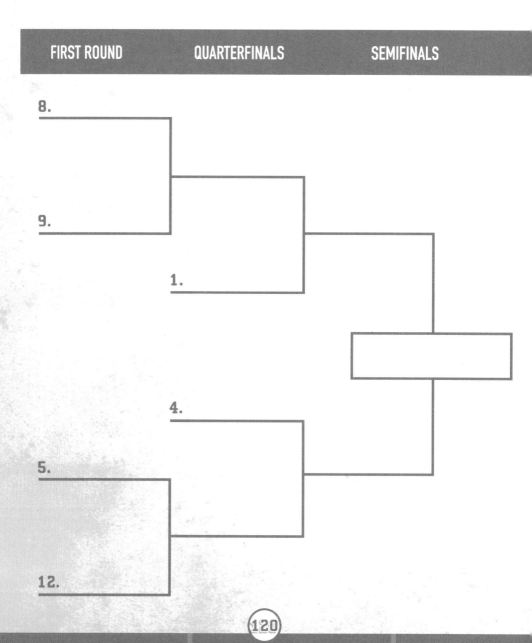

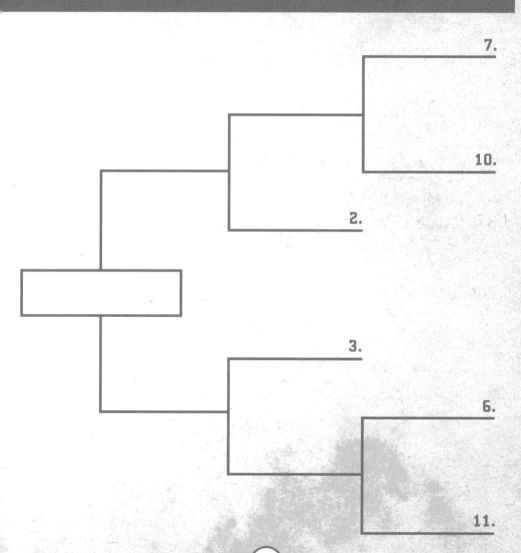

QUARTERFINALS AND SEMIFINALS

Nicknamed the "New Year's Six," six Bowl games are played every season on or around New Year's Day. Beginning in 2024, the Bowls are the quarterfinal and semifinal rounds of the playoffs. Although the Bowls used to have Conference tie-ins, this is no longer necessarily the case—any team can play in any of the Bowls. Fill in the teams who play, and information about these games, on these pages

COTTON BOWL   Round: _____

_____ vs. _____   Date: _____

Location: AT&T STADIUM, ARLINGTON, TEXAS   Weather: _____

Where I watched: _____   Final score: _____

Highlights: _____
_____
_____
_____
_____

FIESTA BOWL

Round: _____

_____ vs. _____   Date: _____

Location: STATE FARM STADIUM, GLENDALE, ARIZONA   Weather: _____

Where I watched: _____   Final score: _____

Highlights: _____

_____

_____

_____

ORANGE BOWL

Round: _____

_____ vs. _____   Date: _____

Location: HARD ROCK STADIUM, MIAMI GARDENS, FLORIDA   Weather: _____

Where I watched: _____   Final score: _____

Highlights: _____

_____

_____

_____

PEACH BOWL Round: _____

_____ vs. _____   Date: _____

Location: MERCEDES-BENZ STADIUM, ATLANTA, GEORGIA   Weather: _____

Where I watched: _____   Final score: _____

Highlights: _____
_____
_____
_____

ROSE BOWL Round: _____

_____ vs. _____   Date: _____

Location: ROSE BOWL STADIUM, PASADENA, CALIFORNIA   Weather: _____

Where I watched: _____   Final score: _____

Highlights: _____
_____
_____
_____

SUGAR BOWL

Round: _____

_____ vs. _____

Date: _____

Location: CAESARS SUPERDOME, NEW ORLEANS, LOUISIANA

Weather: _____

Where I watched: _____

Final score: _____

Highlights: _____
_____
_____

NATIONAL CHAMPIONSHIP GAME

The National Championship Game is played between the two semifinal winners of the playoffs. The game is usually played in late January (more than a week after the semifinal games). The location of the National Championship rotates every year.

_____ vs. _____   Date: _____

Location: _____   Weather: _____

Where I watched: _____   Final score: _____

Highlights: _____
_____
_____
_____
_____

COLLEGE AWARD WINNERS

Fill in your predicted winners on the first line for each award, and the actual winner on the second line. (Did you get them all right?)

Heisman Trophy
(Outstanding Player)
_____
_____

Maxwell Award
(Player of the Year)
_____
_____

Biletnikoff Award
(Outstanding Receiver)
_____
_____

Davey O'Brien Award
(Best Quarterback)
_____
_____

Chuck Bednarik Award
(Defensive Player of the Year)
_____
_____

The Playbook

Ohio State running back Archie Griffin is the only player to win two Heisman Awards. He won them in 1974 and 1975. (Source: Heisman.com)

FOURTH QUARTER

Welcome to the fourth quarter of your journal. Sure, the NFL and college football seasons are big deals, but there *are* other football leagues that demand our attention. High School? The UFL? The CFL? *Yes, please!*

High School Football	**130**
Rivalries	**132**
State Championships	**134**
United Football League	**136**
Canadian Football League	**140**

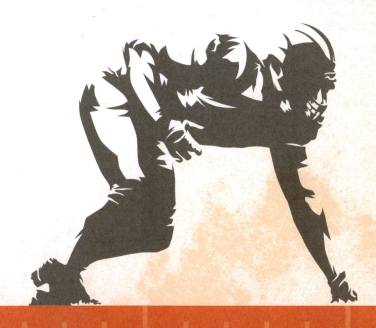

HIGH SCHOOL FOOTBALL

Similar to the NFL and college football, the high school regular season starts in late August, but only runs through November before moving into the playoffs. Each US state has its own rules, but generally, schools are grouped in conferences or divisions and play each other based on size, where they are located, and just how good they are. Each team usually plays about eight to ten regular season games, followed by playoffs (if the team qualifies). Each state names various state champions based on their size.

High school football teams are often the cornerstone of a community. People from all stages of life come out to support their team underneath the Friday night lights or on bright Saturday mornings. Pride in your team—and your town—comes into play during high school matchups!

High School Football Top Teams

Who do you think are some of the top teams in high school football?

_____
_____
_____
_____
_____
_____
_____
_____

High School Mascots

The most common high school football mascot is the eagle, followed by the bulldog. (Source: USA Today) Which mascots represented you in school?

_____
_____

RIVALRIES

High school rivalries are some of the most intense in all of football. One of the most famous rivalries is between Ohio schools Massillon High School and McKinley High School. The schools are just eight miles from each other and the matchup is known as the "War of 1894," because the rivalry dates back to the nineteenth century. Another big rivalry is between Highland Park High School and Plano High School in Texas, the state where football is nearly a second religion. Or how about the Thanksgiving cross-state brawl between Easton High School (Pennsylvania) and Phillipsburg (New Jersey)? Use these pages to jot down some of your favorite high school football memories, especially the rivalries!

Who are some of the best current high school players and/or teams in your area?

_____

_____

_____

_____

_____

_____

_____

Who were the best high school players from your area that went on to play in college? Did any also go pro?

_____

_____

_____

_____

What was the most entertaining high school rivalry in your area?

_____

_____

_____

_____

STATE CHAMPIONSHIPS

For high school players, a state championship game is like the Super Bowl. The number of state football champions varies from state to state. In a big state like California, there are 14 divisions, each with its own state champion. Texas crowns 12 champions, while Pennsylvania crowns just six.

Make note of the high school champions in your state—or the state that you care about the most.

_____

_____

_____

_____

The Playbook

High schools with the most state championship titles:
- Washington High School (Sioux Falls, South Dakota)
- Central High School (Little Rock, Arkansas)
- New Britain High School (Connecticut)
- Artesia High School (New Mexico)
- Lawrence High School (Kansas)   (Source: Maxpreps.com)

My State Championship Game

_____ vs. _____   Location: _____

Date: _____   Where I watched: _____

Weather: _____

How Exciting Was the Game?

① ② ③ ④ ⑤

Final score: _____

ON THE GRIDIRON

- ☐ Kickoff return for a TD
- ☐ 50-yard plus field goal
- ☐ 60-yard plus touchdown run
- ☐ Touchdown dance in end zone
- ☐ Quarterback scrambles for touchdown
- ☐ Quarterback sack and fumble
- ☐ Interception
- ☐ Defensive touchdown

Amazing Plays: _____

Future College Players: _____

Coolest Mascot: _____

UNITED FOOTBALL LEAGUE

The United Football League (UFL) kicked off again in March 2025 for their second season, and a fitting replacement for the Arena Football League (AFL) which played its last season in 2024. The UFL is similar to the NFL and is played on the same size field, but there are only eight teams in the league and there are also some rule differences. For example, after a team scores a touchdown they can go for a one, two, or three point conversion.

UFL Teams

USFL CONFERENCE

Birmingham Stallions
Houston Roughnecks
Memphis Showboats
Michigan Panthers

XFL CONFERENCE

Arlington Renegades
DC Defenders
San Antonio Brahmas
St. Louis Battlehawks

WINNING PREDICTIONS

Who do you think will be the top teams in the league?

USFL Conference Winner: _____

XFL Conference Winner: _____

Best Offense: _____

Best Defense: _____

Best Special Teams: _____

League Champion: _____

UNITED FOOTBALL REGULAR SEASON

The regular season includes a 10-week schedule from March until June. Four teams make the playoffs based on the top two teams in each division. The two divisions are the USFL and the UXL Conference. Record the stats from your favorite game of the season below!

_____ vs. _____   Location: _____

Date: _____   Where I watched: _____

Crowd mood: _____   **How Exciting Was the Game?**
                                        ① ② ③ ④ ⑤

Final score: _____

Amazing Plays: _____

_____

_____

_____

Player of the Game: _____

UFL CHAMPIONSHIP GAME

The championship game is played at a different location every season between two semifinal winners. In 2024, the Birmingham Stallions defeated the San Antonio Brahmas, 25-0. The game had the only shutout of the entire season. Record your reactions below!

_____ vs. _____ Location: _____

Date: _____ Where I watched: _____

Crowd mood: _____

How Exciting Was the Game?
① ② ③ ④ ⑤

Final score: _____

Amazing Plays: _____

_____

_____

_____

Player of the Game: _____

CANADIAN FOOTBALL LEAGUE

The Canadian Football League (CFL) is a professional league in—you guessed it—Canada. The league has nine teams divided into two divisions and the season runs from June to November. The CFL field is larger than the standard NFL field and each team competes with 12 players on the field—one more than in American football. Another difference is that offenses only have three downs—instead of four—to go ten yards (9 m) and achieve a first down. This encourages even more passing plays for more exciting game action!

CFL Teams

EAST DIVISION

Hamilton Tiger-Cats
Montreal Alouettes
Ottawa Redblacks
Toronto Argonauts

Circle your favorite team(s)!

WEST DIVISION

BC Lions
Calgary Stampeders
Edmonton Elks
Saskatchewan Roughriders
Winnipeg Blue Bombers

WINNING PREDICTIONS

Who do you think will be the top teams in the league?

East Division Winner: _____

West Division Winner: _____

Best Offense: _____

Best Defense: _____

Best Special Teams: _____

Grey Cup Champion: _____

CFL REGULAR SEASON

The regular season includes each team playing 18 games over 21 weeks. Teams battle for top standings in either the East or West Division. The top three teams from each division make the playoffs. Take notes on your favorite regular season game you watch!

_____ vs. _____

Location: _____

Date: _____

Where I watched: _____

Crowd mood: _____

How Exciting Was the Game?
① ② ③ ④ ⑤

Final score: _____

Amazing Plays: _____

_____

_____

_____

Player of the Game: _____

THE GREY CUP

The Grey Cup is the championship game of the CFL and one of Canada's biggest sporting events. The Cup was first awarded in 1909 and is usually held every year in late November. The winners of the East and West Division Finals face off in the game known as "Canada's Super Bowl." Similar to the NFL championship, the game takes place in a different Canadian city every year.

_____ vs. _____   Location: _____

Date: _____   Where I watched: _____

Crowd mood: _____   **How Exciting Was the Game?**
① ② ③ ④ ⑤

Final score: _____

Amazing Plays: _____
_____
_____
_____

Player of the Game: _____

OVERTIME

What do you do in the football offseason?
Do you take a break from the sport? We don't think so!
Instead, you keep doing all things football—
besides watching the actual game, of course.
This section is meant to help you do all the football
things you don't have time to do during the season.

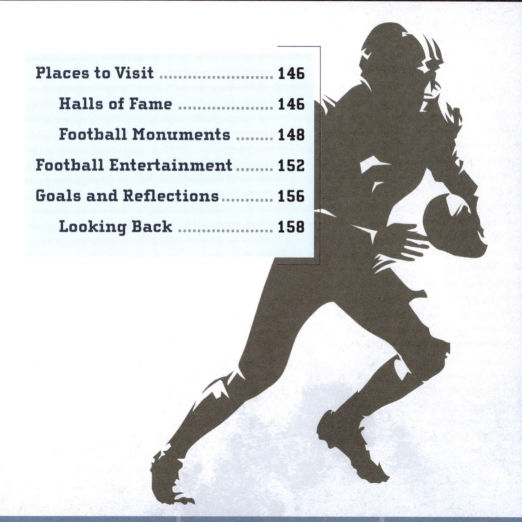

Places to Visit	**146**
Halls of Fame	146
Football Monuments	148
Football Entertainment	**152**
Goals and Reflections	**156**
Looking Back	158

PLACES TO VISIT

Traveling to football destinations brings you a deeper connection to the history of the game. Football museums and monuments celebrate the achievements of legendary players, coaches, and teams. We also left space for you to fill in your own football travel destinations!

Halls of Fame

☐ NFL Hall of Fame, Canton, Ohio

The Pro Football Hall of Fame is a must-visit destination for football fans and history buffs. The Hall was built in 1963 and celebrates the history of professional football, including:

- ☐ **Pro Football Today Gallery,**
  featuring current players and recent seasons
- ☐ **Lamar Hunt Super Bowl Gallery,**
  highlighting Super Bowl memorabilia
- ☐ **Pro Football Hall of Fame Field**
  at Tom Benson Hall of Fame Stadium, which hosts the annual Hall of Fame Game
- ☐ **The Black College Football Hall of Fame**
  is also located within the Pro Football Hall of Fame

Hall of Fame Itinerary

Date: _____

Travel companions: _____

Highlights: _____

Weather: _____

Other activities: _____

☐ College Football Hall of Fame, Atlanta, Georgia

The College Football Hall of Fame, which opened in downtown Atlanta in 2014, offers superfans the chance to celebrate the history and tradition of college football through various displays of memorabilia and important football moments, including:

- ☐ **Interactive Exhibits:**
  Do you want to try calling your own plays or kicking a field goal on a 45-yard (41 m) indoor football field? You can do it all here.
- ☐ **Hall of Fame Rotunda:**
  Check out the names and faces of over 1,000 Hall of Fame inductees here.
- ☐ **Special Exhibits:**
  The Hall regularly hosts rotating exhibits that feature certain teams or players. Make sure to check their website before you go to see what will be there.
- ☐ **Helmet Wall:**
  See the wall that features over 760 school helmets!

Hall of Fame Itinerary

Date: _____

Travel companions: _____

Highlights: _____

Weather: _____

Other activities: _____

Both Halls are typically open daily year-round, but make sure to check their websites for specific closures around holidays or seasons. Plan to spend around two hours exploring the College Hall and to try visit the NFL Hall in August around the time of the Hall of Fame Game and the Enshrinement Ceremony for new inductees.

FOOTBALL MONUMENTS

Traveling across the country to see tributes to football icons is an awesome reason to travel. Here are some monuments to put on your bucket list, plus space to list anything we missed!

Vince Lombardi Statue

Location: outside Lambeau Field in Green Bay, Wisconsin

Honoring Vince Lombardi, the legendary coach of the Green Bay Packers, who led the team to five NFL Championships and the first two Super Bowl titles ever.

Pat Tillman Statue

Location: Arizona State University in Tempe, Arizona

Honoring Pat Tillman, the former Arizona State University and NFL player who left his football career to join the US Army and was killed in action in Afghanistan in 2004.

Manning Monument

Location: outside Lucas Oil Field Stadium in Indianapolis, Indiana

Honoring Hall of Fame quarterback Peyton Manning, who played 11 seasons with the Indianapolis Colts and led them to two Super Bowls and one Super Bowl victory.

Doug Flutie Statue

Location: Boston College in Chestnut Hill, Massachusetts

Honoring Boston College quarterback Doug Flutie and his famous Hail Mary pass in a 1984 game against the University of Miami.

Philly Special Statue

Location: Lincoln Financial Field in Philadelphia, Pennsylvania

Unveiled in 2018, after the Eagles won their first ever Super Bowl title, this statue features quarterback Nick Foles asking his coach if he wants him to do the "Philly Philly," a trick play in which the quarterback catches the ball for a touchdown.
(They did it—and the play worked!)

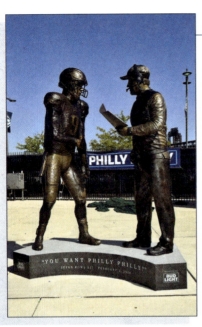

"The Catch"

Location: Levi's Stadium in Santa Clara, California

Captures the moment of "the catch," when Joe Montana of the 49ers threw a game-winning touchdown pass to Dwight Clark in the 1981 NFC Championship game.

Other monuments and destinations I hope to visit:

_____

_____

_____

_____

_____

_____

_____

FOOTBALL ENTERTAINMENT

Football entertainment spans podcasts, movies, television shows, video games, collectibles, and books. All these pieces allow fans to engage with the sport of football beyond the field and enhances the football experience, connecting fans to the sport in even more diverse and immersive ways!

Watch

Football movies and shows capture the drama, excitement, and depth of the sport—and they're also just super fun to watch. Here are some of the best.

Movies

Remember the Titans (2000)
Rudy (1993)
Friday Night Lights (2004)
The Blind Side (2009)
Any Given Sunday (1999)

(Source: *Mountain West Wire*, 2024)

Shows

Friday Night Lights
Last Chance U
Blue Mountain State
Coach

(Source: *Screen Rant*, 2024)

My Favorite Football Movies

_____

_____

_____

_____

_____

My Favorite Football Shows

_____

_____

_____

_____

_____

Listen

Football podcasts offer in-depth analysis, interviews, and discussions on teams, players, and matchups. The best podcasts can be enjoyed by die-hard and casual fans of the sport.

Top Five Most Popular Podcasts

Pardon My Take
New Heights with Jason and Travis Kelce
Josh Pate's College Football Show
The Herd with Colin Cowherd
NFL Daily with Gregg Rosenthal

(Source: Apple Podcasts, 2024)

My Favorite Football Podcasts

_____

_____

_____

_____

_____

_____

_____

Play

Video games allow fans to experience the thrill of football through realistic gameplay, managing teams, and competing in virtual Super Bowls. Feel like you're on the field with these games!

Top-Rated Football Video Games of All Time

ESPN NFL 2K4
Tecmo Super Bowl
NFL Blitz 2000
Madden NFL 2005
NCAA Football 14

(Source: *Bleacher Report*, 2024)

My Favorite Football Video Games

_____

_____

_____

_____

_____

Other Football Entertainment I Want to Check Out

_____

_____

_____

_____

_____

Collect

What is better for a fan than to own a piece of football history celebrating their favorite teams and athletes? Nothing! And some collectibles can be worth a lot of money too!

The Most Valuable Football Memorabilia

2017 Panini National Treasures Platinum Patrick Mahomes 1/1 NFL Shield:
$4.3 million

Tom Brady 2000 Playoff Contenders Championship Ticket Autograph BGS:
$4.3 million

Signed Tom Brady Buccaneers Jersey 2020:
$480,000

Bruce Smith's 1941 Heisman Trophy:
$395,000

(Source: ESPN.com)

My Most Valuable Collectible
_____
_____

My Most Beloved Collectible
_____
_____

My Favorite Bobblehead
_____
_____

My Most Interesting Fan Merchandise
_____
_____

My Favorite Football Card
_____
_____

My Favorite Jersey
_____
_____

GOALS AND REFLECTIONS

We've given you a lot of ways to experience the world as a football fan. What do you hope to do in the next year? What about in the next five years?

(Another) Football Bucket List
Check These Off When You Accomplish Them!

☐ **Attend a Super Bowl** — Date: _____

☐ **Host a Super Bowl Party** — Date: _____

☐ **Get a Selfie with Your Favorite Mascot** — Date: _____

☐ **Get an Autograph from Your Favorite Player** — Date: _____

☐ **Watch Every Game of the Season for Your Favorite Team** — Date: _____

☐ **See an NFL Game Outside North America** — Date: _____

☐ **Attend a College National Championship Game** — Date: _____

☐ **Attend the Grey Cup Championship** — Date: _____

☐ **Attend the ArenaBowl Championship** — Date: _____

☐ **Win Your Fantasy Football League** — Date: _____

LOOKING BACK

Way to go! As a football superfan, you've accomplished so much. You traveled, you cheered, you tasted all kinds of unique and yummy stadium food. After doing and seeing so much, it's a good idea to reflect on your journey. Maybe then you can pass (pun intended) on some of your own tips to future football superfans.
Write down some of your best memories here!

NFL Stadium with the Best Fans _____

_____

_____

_____

_____

College Stadium with the Best Fans _____

_____

_____

_____

_____

The Best Player I Got to See Live _____

_____
_____
_____
_____

The Most Amazing Play I Saw Live _____

_____
_____
_____
_____

**The Longest Football Trip
I Took and What Made It Special** _____

_____
_____
_____
_____

The Craziest Weather I Watched a Game In _____

_____
_____
_____
_____

My Most Treasured Football Gear _____

_____
_____
_____
_____

My Worst Football Day
(Because Sometimes—Rarely—Bad Things
Do Happen in Football) _____

_____
_____
_____
_____

The Best Player I Got to Meet at an NFL Preseason Camp _____

_____

_____

_____

_____

My Most Memorable Tailgate _____

_____

_____

_____

_____

STAT SHEET: GAME ONE

TEAM: _____ QTR ___ : _____

PLAY NO.	PLAY SITUATION BALL ON	DOWN-DISTANCE	RUSH PLYR NO.	YDS.	PASS FROM NO.	TO NO.	YDS.	NOTES
1								
2								
3								
4								
5								
6								
7								
8								
9								
10								
11								
12								
13								
14								
15								
16								
17								
18								
19								
20								
21								
22								
23								
24								
25								
26								
27								
28								
29								
30								
TOTALS THIS QTR.								

1ST DOWNS	1	2	3	4	5	6	7
PASS							
BY RUSH							
BY PENALTY							

TIMEOUTS
1
2
3

PLAY NO.	PENALTIES TEAM	PLYR.	YDS.	TYPE
	NC/OPP			
	NC/OPP			
	NC/OPP			
	NC/OPP			
	NC/OPP			
	NC/OPP			
	NC/OPP			
	NC/OPP			

PLAY NO./CLOCK	TURNOVERS F/INT BY NO.	REC/INT BY NO.	RETURNS FROM YD. LINE	TO YD. LINE	TOTAL YDS.
	F/INT				
	F/INT				
	F/INT				
	F/INT				
	F/INT				
	F/INT				
	F/INT				
	F/INT				

PLAY/CLOCK	TYPE OF KICK	KICKING GAME KICKING TEAM	KICKER NO.	FROM YD. LINE	TO YD. LINE	TOTAL YARDS	RESULT	TEAM	RETURNS PLAYER NO.	FROM YD. LINE	TO YD. LINE	TOTAL YARDS	RESULT
		NC/OPP						NC/OPP					
		NC/OPP						NC/OPP					
		NC/OPP						NC/OPP					
		NC/OPP						NC/OPP					
		NC/OPP						NC/OPP					
		NC/OPP						NC/OPP					
		NC/OPP						NC/OPP					
		NC/OPP						NC/OPP					

OPPONENT: _____ **QTR** ___ : _____

PLAY NO.	PLAY SITUATION		RUSH		PASS			NOTES
	BALL ON	DOWN-DISTANCE	PLYR NO.	YDS.	FROM NO.	TO NO.	YDS.	
1								
2								
3								
4								
5								
6								
7								
8								
9								
10								
11								
12								
13								
14								
15								
16								
17								
18								
19								
20								
21								
22								
23								
24								
25								
26								
27								
28								
29								
30								
TOTALS THIS QTR.								

1ST DOWNS	1	2	3	4	5	6	7
PASS							
BY RUSH							
BY PENALTY							

TIMEOUTS
1
2
3

PLAY NO.	PENALTIES			
	TEAM	PLYR.	YDS.	TYPE
	NC/OPP			
	NC/OPP			
	NC/OPP			
	NC/OPP			
	NC/OPP			
	NC/OPP			
	NC/OPP			
	NC/OPP			

PLAY NO./CLOCK	TURNOVERS		RETURNS		
	F/INT BY NO.	REC/INT BY NO.	FROM YD. LINE	TO YD. LINE	TOTAL YDS.
	F/INT				
	F/INT				
	F/INT				
	F/INT				
	F/INT				
	F/INT				
	F/INT				
	F/INT				

PLAY/CLOCK	KICKING GAME						RETURNS					
	TYPE OF KICK	KICKING TEAM	KICKER NO.	FROM YD. LINE	TO YD. LINE	TOTAL YARDS	RESULT	TEAM	PLAYER NO.	FROM YD. LINE	TO YD. LINE	TOTAL YARDS	RESULT
		NC/OPP						NC/OPP					
		NC/OPP						NC/OPP					
		NC/OPP						NC/OPP					
		NC/OPP						NC/OPP					
		NC/OPP						NC/OPP					
		NC/OPP						NC/OPP					
		NC/OPP						NC/OPP					
		NC/OPP						NC/OPP					

STAT SHEET: GAME TWO

TEAM: _____ QTR ___ : _____

PLAY NO.	PLAY SITUATION		RUSH		PASS		NOTES
	BALL ON	DOWN-DISTANCE	PLYR NO.	YDS.	FROM TO NO. NO.	YDS.	
1							
2							
3							
4							
5							
6							
7							
8							
9							
10							
11							
12							
13							
14							
15							
16							
17							
18							
19							
20							
21							
22							
23							
24							
25							
26							
27							
28							
29							
30							
TOTALS THIS QTR.							

1ST DOWNS	1	2	3	4	5	6	7
PASS							
BY RUSH							
BY PENALTY							

TIMEOUTS
1
2
3

PLAY NO.	PENALTIES			
	TEAM	PLYR.	YDS.	TYPE
	NC/OPP			
	NC/OPP			
	NC/OPP			
	NC/OPP			
	NC/OPP			
	NC/OPP			
	NC/OPP			
	NC/OPP			

PLAY NO./CLOCK	TURNOVERS		RETURNS		TOTAL YDS.
	F/INT BY NO.	REC/INT BY NO.	FROM YD. LINE	TO YD. LINE	
	F/INT				
	F/INT				
	F/INT				
	F/INT				
	F/INT				
	F/INT				
	F/INT				
	F/INT				

PLAY/CLOCK	KICKING GAME						RETURNS				
	TYPE OF KICK	KICKING TEAM	KICKER NO.	FROM YD. LINE	TO YD. LINE	TOTAL YARDS	RESULT	TEAM	PLAYER NO.	FROM YD. LINE	TO YD. LINE	TOTAL YARDS	RESULT
		NC/OPP						NC/OPP					
		NC/OPP						NC/OPP					
		NC/OPP						NC/OPP					
		NC/OPP						NC/OPP					
		NC/OPP						NC/OPP					
		NC/OPP						NC/OPP					
		NC/OPP						NC/OPP					
		NC/OPP						NC/OPP					

OPPONENT: _____ QTR ___ : _____

PLAY NO.	PLAY SITUATION		RUSH		PASS			
	BALL ON	DOWN-DISTANCE	PLYR NO.	YDS.	FROM NO.	TO NO.	YDS.	NOTES
1								
2								
3								
4								
5								
6								
7								
8								
9								
10								
11								
12								
13								
14								
15								
16								
17								
18								
19								
20								
21								
22								
23								
24								
25								
26								
27								
28								
29								
30								
TOTALS THIS QTR.								

1ST DOWNS	1	2	3	4	5	6	7
PASS							
BY RUSH							
BY PENALTY							

TIMEOUTS
1
2
3

PLAY NO.	PENALTIES			
	TEAM	PLYR.	YDS.	TYPE
	NC/OPP			
	NC/OPP			
	NC/OPP			
	NC/OPP			
	NC/OPP			
	NC/OPP			
	NC/OPP			
	NC/OPP			

PLAY NO./CLOCK	TURNOVERS		RETURNS		
	F/INT BY NO.	REC/INT BY NO.	FROM YD. LINE	TO YD. LINE	TOTAL YDS.
	F/INT				
	F/INT				
	F/INT				
	F/INT				
	F/INT				
	F/INT				
	F/INT				

PLAY/CLOCK	KICKING GAME						RETURNS					
	TYPE OF KICK	KICKING TEAM	KICKER NO.	FROM YD. LINE	TO YD. LINE	TOTAL YARDS	RESULT	TEAM	PLAYER NO.	FROM YD. LINE	TO YD. LINE	TOTAL YARDS	RESULT
		NC/OPP						NC/OPP					
		NC/OPP						NC/OPP					
		NC/OPP						NC/OPP					
		NC/OPP						NC/OPP					
		NC/OPP						NC/OPP					
		NC/OPP						NC/OPP					
		NC/OPP						NC/OPP					
		NC/OPP						NC/OPP					

STAT SHEET: GAME THREE

TEAM: _____ QTR ___ : _____

PLAY NO.	PLAY SITUATION			RUSH		PASS			NOTES
	BALL ON	DOWN-DISTANCE	PLYR NO.	YDS.	FROM NO.	TO NO.	YDS.	
1								
2								
3								
4								
5								
6								
7								
8								
9								
10								
11								
12								
13								
14								
15								
16								
17								
18								
19								
20								
21								
22								
23								
24								
25								
26								
27								
28								
29								
30								
TOTALS THIS QTR.								

1ST DOWNS	1	2	3	4	5	6	7
PASS							
BY RUSH							
BY PENALTY							

TIMEOUTS	
1	
2	
3	

PENALTIES			
PLAY NO.	TEAM	PLYR.	YDS.	TYPE
	NC/OPP			
	NC/OPP			
	NC/OPP			
	NC/OPP			
	NC/OPP			
	NC/OPP			
	NC/OPP			
	NC/OPP			

	TURNOVERS		RETURNS		
PLAY NO./CLOCK	F/INT BY NO.	REC/INT BY NO.	FROM YD. LINE	TO YD. LINE	TOTAL YDS.
	F/INT				
	F/INT				
	F/INT				
	F/INT				
	F/INT				
	F/INT				
	F/INT				
	F/INT				

	KICKING GAME						RETURNS				
PLAY/CLOCK	TYPE OF KICK	KICKING TEAM	KICKER NO.	FROM YD. LINE	TO YD. LINE	TOTAL YARDS	RESULT	TEAM	PLAYER NO.	FROM YD. LINE	TO YD. LINE	TOTAL YARDS	RESULT
		NC/OPP						NC/OPP					
		NC/OPP						NC/OPP					
		NC/OPP						NC/OPP					
		NC/OPP						NC/OPP					
		NC/OPP						NC/OPP					
		NC/OPP						NC/OPP					
		NC/OPP						NC/OPP					
		NC/OPP						NC/OPP					

OPPONENT: _____ **QTR** ___ : _____

PLAY NO.	PLAY SITUATION		RUSH		PASS			NOTES
	BALL ON	DOWN-DISTANCE	PLYR NO.	YDS.	FROM NO.	TO NO.	YDS.	
1								
2								
3								
4								
5								
6								
7								
8								
9								
10								
11								
12								
13								
14								
15								
16								
17								
18								
19								
20								
21								
22								
23								
24								
25								
26								
27								
28								
29								
30								
TOTALS THIS QTR.								

1ST DOWNS	1	2	3	4	5	6	7
PASS							
BY RUSH							
BY PENALTY							

TIMEOUTS
1
2
3

PLAY NO.	PENALTIES			
	TEAM	PLYR.	YDS.	TYPE
	NC/OPP			
	NC/OPP			
	NC/OPP			
	NC/OPP			
	NC/OPP			
	NC/OPP			
	NC/OPP			
	NC/OPP			

PLAY NO./CLOCK	TURNOVERS		RETURNS		TOTAL YDS.
	F/INT BY NO.	REC/INT BY NO.	FROM YD. LINE	TO YD. LINE	
	F/INT				
	F/INT				
	F/INT				
	F/INT				
	F/INT				
	F/INT				
	F/INT				
	F/INT				

PLAY/CLOCK	KICKING GAME						RETURNS				
	TYPE OF KICK	KICKING TEAM	KICKER NO.	FROM YD. LINE	TO YD. LINE	TOTAL YARDS	RESULT	TEAM	PLAYER NO.	FROM YD. LINE	TO YD. LINE	TOTAL YARDS	RESULT
		NC/OPP						NC/OPP					
		NC/OPP						NC/OPP					
		NC/OPP						NC/OPP					
		NC/OPP						NC/OPP					
		NC/OPP						NC/OPP					
		NC/OPP						NC/OPP					
		NC/OPP						NC/OPP					

STAT SHEET: GAME FOUR

TEAM: _____ QTR ___ : _____

PLAY NO.	PLAY SITUATION			RUSH		PASS			NOTES
	BALL ON	DOWN-DISTANCE	PLYR NO.	YDS.	FROM NO.	TO NO.	YDS.	
1								
2								
3								
4								
5								
6								
7								
8								
9								
10								
11								
12								
13								
14								
15								
16								
17								
18								
19								
20								
21								
22								
23								
24								
25								
26								
27								
28								
29								
30								
TOTALS THIS QTR.								

1ST DOWNS	1	2	3	4	5	6	7
PASS							
BY RUSH							
BY PENALTY							

TIMEOUTS
1
2
3

PENALTIES

PLAY NO.	TEAM	PLYR.	YDS.	TYPE
	NC/OPP			
	NC/OPP			
	NC/OPP			
	NC/OPP			
	NC/OPP			
	NC/OPP			
	NC/OPP			
	NC/OPP			

PLAY NO./CLOCK	TURNOVERS		RETURNS		
	F/INT BY NO.	REC/INT BY NO.	FROM YD. LINE	TO YD. LINE	TOTAL YDS.
	F/INT				
	F/INT				
	F/INT				
	F/INT				
	F/INT				
	F/INT				
	F/INT				
	F/INT				

KICKING GAME / RETURNS

PLAY/CLOCK	TYPE OF KICK	KICKING TEAM	KICKER NO.	FROM YD. LINE	TO YD. LINE	TOTAL YARDS	RESULT	TEAM	PLAYER NO.	FROM YD. LINE	TO YD. LINE	TOTAL YARDS	RESULT
		NC/OPP						NC/OPP					
		NC/OPP						NC/OPP					
		NC/OPP						NC/OPP					
		NC/OPP						NC/OPP					
		NC/OPP						NC/OPP					
		NC/OPP						NC/OPP					
		NC/OPP						NC/OPP					
		NC/OPP						NC/OPP					

OPPONENT: _____ **QTR** ___ : _____

PLAY NO.	PLAY SITUATION		RUSH		PASS			NOTES
	BALL ON	DOWN-DISTANCE	PLYR NO.	YDS.	FROM NO.	TO NO.	YDS.	
1								
2								
3								
4								
5								
6								
7								
8								
9								
10								
11								
12								
13								
14								
15								
16								
17								
18								
19								
20								
21								
22								
23								
24								
25								
26								
27								
28								
29								
30								
TOTALS THIS QTR.								

1ST DOWNS	1	2	3	4	5	6	7
PASS							
BY RUSH							
BY PENALTY							

TIMEOUTS	
1	
2	
3	

PENALTIES					
PLAY NO.	TEAM	PLYR.	YDS.	TYPE
	NC/OPP			
	NC/OPP			
	NC/OPP			
	NC/OPP			
	NC/OPP			
	NC/OPP			
	NC/OPP			
	NC/OPP			

	TURNOVERS		RETURNS		
PLAY NO./CLOCK	F/INT BY NO.	REC/INT BY NO.	FROM YD. LINE	TO YD. LINE	TOTAL YDS.
	F/INT				
	F/INT				
	F/INT				
	F/INT				
	F/INT				
	F/INT				
	F/INT				

	KICKING GAME						RETURNS				
PLAY/CLOCK	TYPE OF KICK	KICKING TEAM	KICKER NO.	FROM YD. LINE	TO YD. LINE	TOTAL YARDS	RESULT	TEAM	PLAYER NO.	FROM YD. LINE	TO YD. LINE	TOTAL YARDS	RESULT
		NC/OPP						NC/OPP					
		NC/OPP						NC/OPP					
		NC/OPP						NC/OPP					
		NC/OPP						NC/OPP					
		NC/OPP						NC/OPP					
		NC/OPP						NC/OPP					
		NC/OPP						NC/OPP					
		NC/OPP						NC/OPP					

AUTOGRAPHS

AUTOGRAPHS

AUTOGRAPHS

AUTOGRAPHS

ACKNOWLEDGMENTS

I have kept a daily journal since I was in the fourth grade, so I feel lucky to have this opportunity to write this unique journal that combines my love of writing with my passion for football.

I can't thank my team at Quarto enough—including my editors Katie McGuire (a meticulous planner and reviser) and Cara Donaldson (a wordsmith and fellow Eagles fan—go Birds!) and the copy editors, proofreaders, and amazing design team who made this book look so accessible and fantastic.

This journal is for everybody who loves the game as much as I do and will use it to create a space to capture their experiences, dreams, and football adventures. Football memories are worth recording and celebrating. I hope this journal provides a perfect place to do just that.

IMAGE CREDITS

Page 148 (top): © Raymond Boyd/Getty Images

Page 148 (bottom): © Gene Lower/Getty Images

Page 148 (top): © 4k-Clips/Alamy Stock Photo

Page 149 (bottom): © Icon Sportswire/Getty Images

Page 150 (top): © Kris Connor/Getty Images

Page 150 (bottom): © Boston Globe/Getty Images

ABOUT THE AUTHOR

Ellen Labrecque grew up outside Philadelphia as a member of a die-hard Eagles family. She now lives in a split home with a New York sports fans. Her husband is an avid baseball and football card collector (a rookie Joe Montana is his most beloved card). An athlete herself (although not football), Ellen played basketball and lacrosse in college. She has since retired her high-tops and cleats for running sneakers.

Ellen has written more than 100 nonfiction books for children. She has authored 13 biographies in *The New York Times* bestselling *Who Was. . . ?* biography series, including one on Travis Kelce. She enjoys exploring various topics and has channeled this research into other books on sports, outer space, animals, jungles, and the environment. This is her first journal to be published.

Ellen was a writer and editor at *Sports Illustrated Kids* magazine for nine years, writing profiles on athletes and covering the Olympics and other sporting events. She now writes from her Bucks County, Pennsylvania, home with her family and her dog, Oscar (a definite Eagles fan).

To my siblings, Billy, Katy, and Patrick, and our mom and dad and their original Eagles group, who all taught me what it means to be a true football fan.
Fly, Eagles, Fly.

© 2025 by Quarto Publishing Group USA Inc.

First published in 2025 by Epic Ink, an imprint of The Quarto Group, 142 West 36th Street, 4th Floor, New York, NY 10018, USA (212) 779-4972 • www.Quarto.com

All rights reserved. No part of this book may be reproduced in any form without written permission of the copyright owners. All images included in this book are original works created by the artist credited on the copyright page, not generated by artificial intelligence, and have been reproduced with the knowledge and prior consent of the artist. The producer, publisher, and printer accept no responsibility for any infringement of copyright or otherwise arising from the contents of this publication. Every effort has been made to ensure that credits accurately comply with information supplied. We apologize for any inaccuracies that may have occurred and will resolve inaccurate or missing information in a subsequent reprinting of the book.

Epic Ink titles are also available at discount for retail, wholesale, promotional, and bulk purchase. For details, contact the Special Sales Manager by email at specialsales@quarto.com or by mail at The Quarto Group, Attn: Special Sales Manager, 100 Cummings Center Suite 265D, Beverly, MA 01915 USA.

10 9 8 7 6 5 4 3 2 1

ISBN: 978-0-7603-9449-6

Group Publisher: Rage Kindelsperger
Creative Director: Laura Drew
Managing Editor: Cara Donaldson
Editor: Katie McGuire
Editorial Assistant: Chloe Gerhard
Text: Ellen Labrecque
Cover Design: Scott Richardson
Interior Design: Foltz Design

Printed in China